Learning Tree
1 2 3

Water

By Susan Baker
Illustrated by Bernard Robinson

CHERRYTREE BOOKS

Read this book and see if you can do the experiments and
answer the questions. Ask an adult or an older friend to
tell you if your answers are right or to help you if you find
the questions difficult. Often there is more than one
answer to a question.
Be very careful with water. It can be dangerous. Never try
to swim unless there is an adult with you. Never put your
hands in hot water. Keep well away from pans and
steaming kettles. Steam is very hot. Even ice can 'burn'.

A Cherrytree Book

Designed and produced by
A S Publishing

First published 1991
by Cherrytree Press Ltd
a subsidiary of
The Chivers Company Ltd
Windsor Bridge Road
Bath, Avon BA2 3AX

Copyright © Cherrytree Press Ltd 1991

British Library Cataloguing in Publication Data
Baker Susan 1942-
    Water
    1. Water
    I. Title   II. Robinson, Bernard 1930-   III. Series
    553.7

    ISBN 0-7451-5152-3

Printed and bound in Italy by L.E.G.O. s.p.a., Vicenza

What will happen if you forget to water your
plants? Will they die?
Nothing can live without water.
Without water there would be no plants.
There would be no animals and no people.

We drink water. We wash in it.
We cook with it. We clean with it.
Can you think of other ways we use it?

4

Do you know how much water there is?
Three-quarters of the world is covered by sea.
Three-quarters of your body is made of water.

Water does not always look the same.
You can see the water that you drink.
You can see water that is frozen.
But sometimes you cannot see water.

There is water in the air all around us.
But we cannot see it because it is a gas.
Water in the air is called water vapour.
Where did the puddle in the picture go?

7

Water is made of lots of tiny particles.
They are called molecules.
When water gets very cold it turns to ice.
The molecules move closer together.
When water turns to gas they move apart.

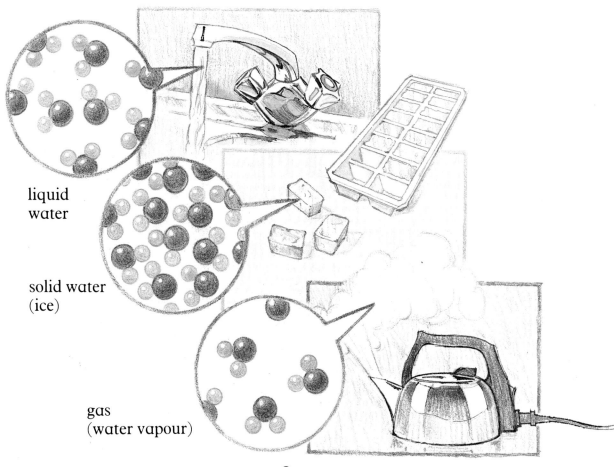

liquid
water

solid water
(ice)

gas
(water vapour)

When you boil water it bubbles and steams.
It gets so hot that it turns to gas.
But the air around it is cool.
The cold air makes the steam turn back into
liquid water.
Never go near a pan of boiling water.

9

When you have a bath does the mirror get steamed up?
Can you think why it does?

Leave some water in a saucer in a warm room.
See how long it takes to dry up.
See how long it takes in a cold room.
You cannot see the dried up water.
But it is there. It is in the air.
See how long it takes the washing to dry.

The sun dries the water on top of the sea.
It turns it to water vapour.
The vapour rises and turns into clouds.
Clouds are made of little drops of water.
They are like the steam in the bathroom.

Rain falls from the clouds on to the land.
The water drains into rivers.
The rivers flow back to the sea.
Water goes round and round and round.
It goes from sea to sky to land to sea.

You can make things disappear with water.
Put a spoonful of salt in a glass of water.

Watch to see what happens.
Can you see the salt? Can you taste it?

The salt has not gone away.
It has dissolved.

Leave some salty water in a saucer.
See what is left when the water dries up.

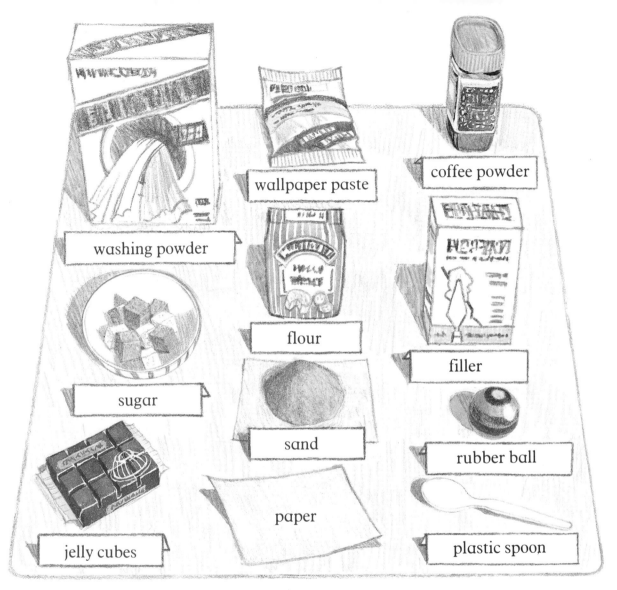

Mix other things with water.
See if they change or stay the same.
Does it make a difference if the water is hot?

16

What happens if you leave a book or a bicycle out in the rain?

Do you know why ships float?
Take two sheets of tin foil the same size.
Fill a bowl of water.

Fold one piece of foil into a tight pack.
Crumple the other into a loose ball.
Drop them gently on to the water.
Which one sinks?

Which of these float in water?
Guess which ones will before you try them.

tomato

salt

carrot

grapes

tangerine

cork

potato

lemon

walnut

ice cube

Put more and more salt in the water and try
the things again.

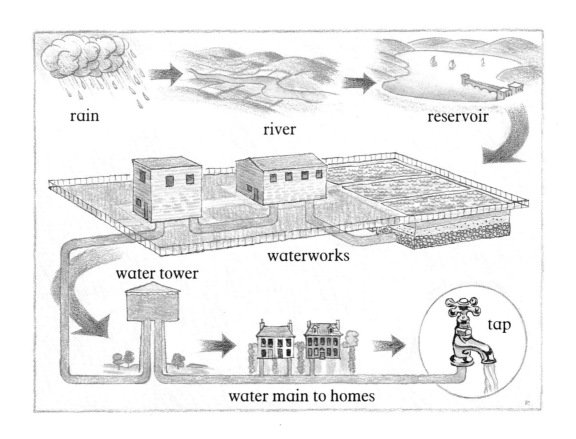

rain

river

reservoir

waterworks

water tower

water main to homes

tap

We use lots of water every day.
The water we drink comes from a tap.
It is clean and fresh.
It has been cleaned at the waterworks.
But once it was dirty rainwater.
Find out how water gets to your home.

20

More about water

Kinds of water
Water can be a gas, a liquid or a solid. It can also be salty or fresh. The water that falls as rain is fresh. The water in the sea is salty. Water from the surface of the sea *evaporates*. It turns to vapour and rises to make clouds. The salt is left behind in the sea.

Some animals and plants can live in salt water. Others can live only in fresh water. People cannot drink salt water. It makes them sick and can kill them.

Irrigation
Crops cannot grow without water. The first people to grow crops made their homes in river valleys where there was plenty of water. They found ways of taking water to fields that were not close to the river. They *irrigated* them. Today we build big dams across rivers so that we can store water to irrigate dry lands.

Water power
Water is heavy and powerful. It moves downhill all the time. It always finds it own level. The weight, or pressure, of water is used to drive machines. It can turn wheels. Big wheels, called turbines, inside dams are driven by water forcing its way through openings in the dam. The turbines produce electricity.

Steam is also powerful. The first trains had steam engines. Factories used steam to power machines. Some power stations use steam to make electricity.

Buoyed up!
Water holds things up, so boats and ships can travel on it. It is *buoyant*. Salt water is more buoyant than fresh water. That is why it is easier to swim in the sea than in a pool.

What a soak!
What do you do when water spills? What do you use to mop it up? Have you noticed how well sponges and cloths soak up water? Half fill a bowl with water. Dangle a piece of wool or string (not nylon) over the side, so that one end is in the water and the other is below the level of the water. See what happens.

21

1

1 Could you live without water?

2 How much of your body is made of water?

3 What is ice?

4 Can you always see water?

5 What happens to water when it boils?

6 What happens to steam when it cools?

2

7 Does sugar dissolve more easily in cold water or in hot?

8 Does water have to boil to turn into a gas?

9 What is *evaporation?*

10 A plant's roots hold it in the ground. What else do they do?

11 All our food and everything we drink has water in it. How many glasses or cups of water do you drink each day?

12 How does water get things clean?

13 Is hot or cold water better for cleaning? Why do you need washing-up liquid to wash dirty plates?

14 Find out what happens to water after it has gone down the drain.

3

15 Make a science notebook. Write in it the answers to these questions and any questions that you want answered. Write about your experiments and other things that you notice about water.

16 Fill an ice tray to the top with water. Look at the frozen cubes. Are they flat or do they stick up over the top of the tray? What has happened?

17 Why do ice cubes float?

18 Which would be best for mopping up water: a flannel, a plastic bag, a sheet of paper?

19 Make a boat from some modelling clay. Make sure that it can float. Then roll the boat back into a ball and try to float it. Does it sink? Find out why the same piece of clay floats one moment and sinks the next.

20 Get two buckets and a length of tubing through which you can suck up water. Fill one bucket with water. See if you can transfer water from one bucket to the other using only the tube.

21 What is a *syphon*?

22 The surface of still water is always flat but the sea has waves. What causes the waves?

23 What is *hydroelectricity*?

24 How long could you last without water: a year, a month, a week, less than a week?

25 An insect called a pond skater walks on the surface of the water. Find out why it can.

26 What is the meaning of *surface tension*?

Index

air 7, 11
animals 3, 21
bath 10
bicycle 17
boat 23
body 5, 22
boiling water 9, 22
book 17
bubbles 9
buoyancy 21
cleaning 4, 22
clouds 12, 13, 21
cold 8, 11, 22
cooking 4
cooling 9, 22
crops 21
dams 21
dissolving 15
drain 22
drinking 4, 6, 20, 22
drying up 11, 12, 15
electricity 21
evaporation 21, 22
floating 18, 19, 23
food 22
fresh water 20, 21
frozen water 6, 8, 23
gas 7, 8, 9, 21, 22
hot 9, 16, 22
how much water 5

hydroelectricity 23
ice 8, 19, 22, 23
irrigation 21
jelly cubes 16
land 13
life 3, 21, 22, 23
liquid water 8, 9, 21
machines 21
mixing 16
molecules 8
mopping up 23
notebook 23
people 3, 21
plants 3, 21
pond skater 23
power station 21
pressure 21
questions 22, 23
rain 13, 17, 20
reservoir 20
rivers 13, 20, 21
roots 22
salt 14, 19
salt water 21
sea 5, 12, 13, 21
sinking 18, 23
sky 13
soaking up 21
solid 8
steam 9, 10, 12, 22

steam engines 21
sugar 16, 22
surface tension 23
syphon 23
tap 20
tin foil 18
turbines 21
uses of water 4
warm 11
washing 4, 11
washing up 22
water level 21
water main 20
water power 21
water tower 20
water vapour 7, 12
waterworks 20
waves 23